I Can Hear

Julie Murray

Abdo
SENSES
Kids

abdopublishing.com

Published by Abdo Kids, a division of ABDO, PO Box 398166, Minneapolis, Minnesota 55439. Copyright © 2016 by Abdo Consulting Group, Inc. International copyrights reserved in all countries. No part of this book may be reproduced in any form without written permission from the publisher.

Printed in the United States of America, North Mankato, Minnesota.

052015

092015

 THIS BOOK CONTAINS RECYCLED MATERIALS

Photo Credits: iStock, Shutterstock

Production Contributors: Teddy Borth, Jennie Forsberg, Grace Hansen

Design Contributors: Candice Keimig, Dorothy Toth

Library of Congress Control Number: 2014958409

Cataloging-in-Publication Data

Murray, Julie.

 I can hear / Julie Murray.

  p. cm. -- (Senses)

ISBN 978-1-62970-925-3

Includes index.

1. Ear--Juvenile literature.   I. Title.

612.8'5--dc23

       2014958409

Table of Contents

I Can Hear

There are five senses.

Hearing is one of the senses.

We hear with our ears.

We hear **sounds** all around us!

We hear loud **sounds**.

Molly hears the train.

We hear **quiet sounds**.

Ethan hears a whisper.

We hear laughter.

Alex makes us laugh.

13

We hear music.

Beth likes to sing.

We hear animals.

The dog **barks**.

We hear our family.

We talk at dinner.

What **sounds** did you

hear today?

The Five Senses

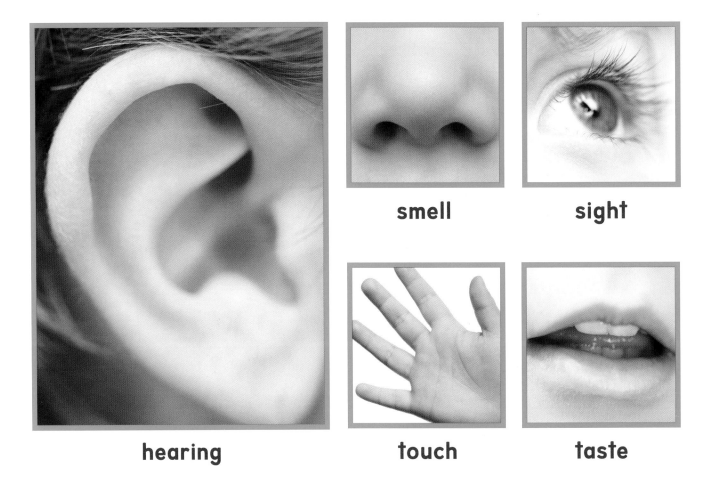

hearing

smell

sight

touch

taste

Glossary

bark
the noise a dog makes.

quiet
a soft noise. Not loud.

sound
a noise that you can hear.

Index

abdokids.com

Use this code to log on to abdokids.com and access crafts, games, videos, and more!

Abdo Kids Code:
SIK9253